CONVERSATION WITH BIO YOGI

In Quest of Self

Anita Sharma

Published by
Delta Book World
New Delhi – 110 002 (India)

In Association with
S. D. Public School
Delhi–110 034 (India)

CONVERSATION WITH BIO YOGI: In Quest of Self

Anita Sharma

First Published in 2023

ISBN: 978-81-959111-9-6

Price: Rs. 199.00

Published by

Delta Book World

G-4, Prahlad House

4832/24, Ansari Road, Darya Ganj

New Delhi – 110 002 (India)

Tel.: 011-4707 2321, Mob: 96542 86004

Email: deltabookworld@gmail.com

In Association with

Mrs. Anita Sharma, Principal

S. D. Public School

Pitampura, Delhi - 110 034

PRINTED IN INDIA

Preface

Every human being on this earth embaks his journey with a struggle by inhaling air into his lungs. During the process, he lets out a loud cry and his whimper brings a smile to the faces of his parents and kin. His cry is an assurance of life and is a reason to celebrate. Newborn cries, smiles, navigates through different phases of life and develops aspirations leading to new destinations and sometimes this search for new destinations converts into the quest for his real self. As the flames quench, life takes new turns and one's consciousness oscillates between the feelings of self and cosmos. Cosmic energy in this movement facilitates the interaction of awakening rising souls with enlightened souls to guide them in the right direction and to lead them towards the eternal truth.

In this journey of inner to infinite two experiences come very naturally, one of them is a connection with enlightened divine souls and yogis and the other is the call from the Himalayas.

The peaks of the Himalayas attract every person who is in search of his own peak and is traveling the distance of his Inner to Eternal. For him "Aham Brhamsami" is not a verse but the metaverse where existence is possible when one unites with the Universal energy.

One such soul moved from Serbia to France. Attaining all material achievements at a very young age a question pinched him, "What next?"

A series of questions started bothering him – Who am I, What am I, Why am I?

This Quest of I landed scientist Milovan Stankov in contact with Maharishi Mahesh Yogi. His guidance transcended him and his journey towards self began. On this journey, one natural halt was the Himalayans. The divine energy of the Himalayans binds and liberates. The energy liberates the ego and conveys the message to liberate others. The energy binds and inspires us to be more dutiful and responsible towards the responsibilities assigned by Cosmic Energy and sweetly whispers the invitation for a return at regular intervals to gather more energy. The connection with divine souls and divine energy transformed scientist Milovan to Yogi Milovan.

One fine day the vibrations of young energies of Sanatan Dharam Public School situated at Pitampura, Delhi touched the Yogi and invited him to the school for interaction. The interaction with students of the school became a regular part of Yogi Milovan's Bharat Yatras. The sequel of interactions between students and Bio Yogi are presented in this book in the form of questions and answers. The interaction of Scientist-Yogi Milovan with students was always enlightening and enriching. The new name coined by the young seekers for Yogi Milovan is BIO YOGI.

The purpose of writing this book is to reach many young minds who are in the quest for truth and self. The purpose is also to reach many "Siddh Purushas" and enlighten divine souls and invite them for conversation with the young curious minds and to steer them in the proper direction. Upanishads emphasize "Encourage Questioning". Getting answers to the doubts and questions raised by young curious minds may lead young seekers on the path of Ecstasy. I hope this book will be helpful to all readers in some or the other way. The major part of the book encapsulates the conversation between young students and Bio Yogi. 'Seeker' is used for all curious minds.

Mrs. Anita Sharma, Principal
S. D. Public School,
Pitampura, Delhi

Contents

Transformative Experiences

After 25 years of regularly coming to India. What to say? I have visited almost all parts of the country from Mumbai to Bénarès and Calcutta, from Delhi to Pondichéry. From Srinagar Matha to Jyotir Matha. From the source of the Ganges to its delta in the Bay of Bengal. I have seen the people, the customs, culture, tradition, monuments, temples, ashrams...all united in diversities, colors, and beauty...The place where I stayed most is the Tapovan plateau, above the Gomukh glacier, at an altitude reaching nearly 4500 m.

There, is just a wave of peace, wild nature, cold river Akash Ganga, few yogis in the caves, a sound and chilly wind, penetrating sunlight, the bright sky in the night full of stars, and an awesome awareness, purna... uniting this tiny planet and everything on it with the Universe. Incredible feeling, the joy of expansion... that literally blew up my petty mind once forever, leaving no more space for "I" or me or a body... infinite freedom, access to all resources, profound vibrant silence, a source of everything and anything...

That's India for me, a type of experience available only there.

Yes, I have also visited most of the continents and the countries of the world, met different people, cultures, traditions, and historical and cultural heritage. I gather all the experiences of the world and I bring to Tapovan once per year to a summit with me and nature, where we sort everything, try to understand human suffering, and advocate peace in the world, looking for "Vasudhaiva Kutumbakam", and after all, I was just learning and growing in the knowledge of my own self. The journey was not in time or in space, the journey was from ignorance to knowledge up to the realization of purna as infinity and the only reality.

–Milovan

1

Celebrating the Mother Language ......

Message on Sanskrit Diwas to Students of Sanatan Dharam Public School, Pitampura, Delhi by Bio Yogi Milovan

Seeker: We are celebrating Sanskrit Diwas in school on Monday i.e. on Aug 3, 2015. Celebrating the day of our seed language is one way to remind the youth about the significance of the language. What is your message on this occasion for the students?

Bio Yogi: The significance of language is the mark of civilization. Scientists have identified a specific gene labeled as "Foxp2", given only to the human species among all living creatures. It allows us to speak, learn, and consciously associate phenomena to create a sensible interpretation. Humans are the only creatures that can communicate using syllables and create words, sentences, and ideas that drive their lives. Since the advent of language human life has grown more socially and culturally dominated, and controlled biologically in comparison to animal species. In other words, biological tradition or transmission of information has been superseded by that of cultural tradition.

Cultural transmission (tradition) of information becomes the main factor in the future evolution of mankind today. If that process becomes interrupted just in one generation, mankind will regress thousands of years back. Language, by its sound and meaning value, cultivates the neuro-physiology of the human brain individually and socially.

Essentially language is a sound, frequency, and vibration in its nature. It is a science of sound (mantras) and carrying energy that produces effects on physiology and the environment (Yagna). It is a known fact that we can create or destroy, program, and control the human mind. And this is what civilization has been doing all the time. But the beauty of what nature has entrusted in us is that we can sing, write poems, express our feelings, and love to relate with each other and with nature. We are the only creatures on this planet who are aware that it has been created. And the only creatures that can express their gratitude and recognition to the creator, dedicating their lives, prayers, and singing to the core of their existence. Sanskrit language is unique in this respect. It is a seed language of all, and a language of pure universal, unity consciousness. By using it in any prescribed form it has the potential to fully unfold the potential of the human brain to function in perfect harmony with nature and to be all time innovative and creative. Sanskrit can empower the human mind to that of the creator. At the same time it provides knowledge and a structure of consciousness on both the unmanifest and manifest levels. The silent level of consciousness, gained through regular meditation, that re-vibrates (hams) within itself is the source of all sounds – the Vedas (Rig-Veda), infinite correlating, omnipresent and omnipotent reality at the basis of creation. Sanskrit chanting and performances establish one in that reality, fully awakened within itself where consciousness fully knows itself. Sanskrit should be taught in every educational instititION around the world since it has the potential of cultivating the human brain to its highest. It is a Heritage of Humanity. So enjoy your celebration, learn 10 Sanskrit words per day, meditate regularly and be grateful and feel graceful to be born as a human being. Do not miss or mess up your chance.

2

Reflections on Self in the Current Discourse: A Conversation with Bio-Yogi

Q 1. Seeker: Namaskar Sir (with folded hands)

We do namaskar with folded hands and bow our heads and convey that I am not ego and 'I' submit to the infinite unlimited God consciousness in the form of you.

How do the people in France convey this?

Bio Yogi: Unfortunately, in the West, this kind of awareness is not there. People salute each other outwardly without any recognition of the reality that dwells within. Ego has stepped in, in all relationships interplaying essential values of life. I salute you with respect as my own self.

Q 2. Seeker: I am keen to know why your email id has Ramraj with Milovan.

What is your interpretation of Ram and Raj?

Is it Lord Rama as Raja (King) or Reign of King Rama or the ideal state where everyone is consciously awakened?

Bio Yogi: Ramraj is that state of consciousness – fully awakened within itself – in which the ruler and the ruled are essentially the same in nature. Matter and the Spirits are one. Whether you are ruled by a mind or by a body or by somebody, you remain the same. Roles are just for the sake of joyful play. If this truth is not realized, established, and lived, play becomes a painful learning process in life.

Q 3. Seeker: Once, the Ramraj is attained there is no worry, no failure, no success, no happiness, and no sorrow. If the ultimate goal of life is to attain the state of Ram, why God has not constituted every human being that way? Why God has sent a semi-finished product on earth and left the rest of the work on this half-finished product to complete himself/herself? GOD is considered perfect. While we human beings are expected to do every work with 100% perfection.

(1) Why should one work for self-development?

(2) What is success?

Bio Yogi (laughing): God is within us, as our real nature, is already in the fully awakened state at all times, guiding our individual awareness to its infinite and unlimited state. As the mother cares for her child. The mother enjoys each step of progress although the child is falling and crying, with the mother's attention it gets up, learns, and continues. We are all already in a state of perfection infused with the universe. We are made out of it. Universe expresses its values and potential through each observable and unobservable form. The universe works through us. But because of our limited individual awareness and its identification with the objects of perception including our mind and body, individuals get conditioned by their attachments to phenomena that catch their perception. In reality, there is nowhere to go, nothing to see, nothing to seek, there is no truth to find, no path to follow, no place to hide. It is unity. Unity is the only reality. Ramraj. You and you alone are one and inseparable, indivisible from the universe. There is nothing to achieve, just to realize the Truth of it through direct experience of consciousness in its totality and observe how it works and unfolds. To explore a kingdom of heaven internally and outwardly. This indeed is real joy and fulfillment. However tender minds do not understand that process, and their rulers do neither. So we have a situation today that a blind guides a blind. You are Ramraj, a Ram, and a Raja for yourself at the same time. As a mind and body are inseparable a ruler and a ruled, a king and a kingdom (a government and a people) are inseparable, dynamic, and interactive reality interplay. Ramayana is a story of you, each of us, and humanity. It is a recipe for achieving a dynamically balanced state of consciousness on an individual and a collective level at both material and spiritual levels. Meditation is a mediation between Ram-mind (individual or collective, or cosmic) and Raj-body (body of the individuals or body of the country, or that of the universe) a learning process of both, the time-changing values of life and universe, assuring their balanced simultaneous growth. This is a real success. To realize and to live that you are cosmic in nature.

Q 4. Seeker: Which aspect of human life is most essential– social, political, religious, or spiritual?

How religion is different from spiritualism in your opinion?

Is having faith in religious beliefs the first step towards a spiritual lifestyle?

Bio Yogi: Our needs define what is essential for us. Essential is existential. I remember I was 25 when this question rose in my mind. I had just started to lead my life independently and was proud to define my own rules and guidelines for my future life. It was a clear cutoff insight: to lead my life I do not need any of these conventional values, neither political nor social nor religious. I have never heard people saying they have political or social or religious needs the same way as they say that they need food or shelter or clothes. To survive I needed only me, myself at every moment, with each breath. And it is still the same. It was this practical approach that really turned me towards the knowledge and experience of my essential and existential nature, creation, and consciousness itself. That was the beginning I believe of myself awakened spiritual journey, that I did not ask for. I remember how much I was torched by these conventional values for so long time, and took me a while to root this burden out of my mind. Of course, I had to understand them fully before hand and to learn why they are there in the first place, many of them to transform and integrate, and most of them I had to discard and throw out of my mind as mental pollutants.

Conventional values demand individuals to conform to them not to challenge, or evolve them.

As a biologist, I appreciated the creativity of nature that expresses itself in a very unique way in all forms that it does and still does through evolution. In each form, individuals are unique and that uniqueness is the key to evolution, not the conformity to either religious or social prototype models, established by religious or social authority (media).

The creation is in charge of you all the time and it works and expresses itself through you. It is a truth that matters all others are just side effects of the human mind accumulated through history as a social and religious value that undergoes the changes all the time.

So go by you, your uniqueness your real needs, and cultivate the humanity in the life and the life in humanity.

Q 5. Seeker: The very thought of taking charge of one's life independently excites youth. But how one can judge whether the path he is adopting is right or wrong? Because when one is not adhering to traditional beliefs he has to live under the pressure of society and somewhere somehow the efforts are made by everybody around to bring back the person to the conformed values. If a person is strong enough to withstand all storms he can step forward. But the problem is that in this situation the person should be determined and fearless. It has always surprised me that all good people bear a sense of fear and are not able to gather courage while all bad people (who are threats to humanity) are daring and fearless. How a person can overcome fear?

Bio Yogi: One should not judge the path he treads. It is of no use. Judgment is on the basis of the knowledge of the past. A path that one undertakes is leading him to the future that unfolds inner potentials hidden within. Its like the growth of a tree from a seed. The problem is that we do not know what kind of "tree" we are and what kind of fruits we should bear. Right or wrong should be weighed based on usefulness. If it proves to be the opposite we change the course. Conventional values offer ready-to-use answers based on the past, but could not lead individuals to themselves, to discover and unfold their inner unique expression of the Oneness. None of these conventional values have an answer about you as you are. One has to raise a question about him/herself and find out the answer by him/her self. If you do not pose a question, nothing is going to happen to you. You will just follow the crowd, repeating and reproducing the values of the past. Nothing wrong with that. It's a choice. This is how society stands today. Individuals can comfortably live their lives in conformity with traditional values. No desire, no knowledge, no true action only reactions to what is there. The questions are the trick of the mind. The questions divide and are a source of progress and fear at the same time, which eventually can lead to the realization of the truth. Individuals (in divided duals) are acting on the basis of their desires, their knowledge, and the fruits of their actions. If the desires of your school/students are treated as your personal desires then you will do everything to fulfill them through your actions. If the desires of the nation become your desires then you will certainly act with courage and fearlessness like Gandhi and APJ Abdul Kalam did in their life times. There is nothing to lose because we do not possess anything. When this is realized then the source of fear vanishes. We are sustained by the creation, a much bigger reality than our petty egoistic mind. True knowledge gained through direct experience of oneself (Ved) through meditation is the only cure for this human-mind disease.

Q 6. Seeker: Swami Ramakrishna Paramhansa was the Guru of Swami Vivekananda. He said that–

> "Purity of mind is an essential condition for the attainment of the Ultimate Reality; real purity is freedom from lust and greed. External observances are only of secondary importance."

How do you define the purity of mind? Why it is essential to know the ultimate YOU?

Bio Yogi: A pure mind is an innocent mind, a mind of a child. A pure innocent (childlike) mind of an enlightened person (that freed its mind from all attachments, all knowledge, and all impressions) is fully awakened within itself. In that state consciousness fully knows its own nature. Ultimate You is a truth of it.

Q 7. Seeker: A child's mind is free from all attachments and impressions because it has no impression or less impression. We had a workshop in school where our eminent speaker shared that a test was done on a group of 5 years old children to assess their creative abilities. The result was 98%. 5 years hence again the test was done on the same group, the result was 40 %that means in a group where 98 out of 100 were displaying creative fervor now just 40 were reflecting this ability. After another 5 years, the results reduced to 20%. That means a soul which is pure and creative when encounters educational experiences and social experiences start polluting and stale. It means we need to think seriously about the education happening in schools and the kind of revamping it requires.

What do you think about the education system and education process in this context?

Bio Yogi: You are fully right. Your speaker brought to your attention a well-known fact across the globe, that current education is a frustration and a total failure everywhere in the world. Only 10 to 20 % of all students end up with high educational degrees and a lot of stress accumulated in their physiology. This is the world we created and live in. What we sow is what we will reap.

The purpose of education is to develop the total potential of human brain physiology while cultivating it to maintain its pure, innocent, innovative, and creative state at its highest potential. Unless the direct experience of pure consciousness (a ground state of reality) through meditation is not a part of the educational system, education will continue to be a source of impediments to human consciousness development globally. Fortunately, I was exposed to the great wisdom of Vedic knowledge and procedures by Maharishi Mahesh Yogi in 1980. He addresses this issue by implementing Transcendental Meditation and the knowledge of consciousness-based education in the educational system across the globe. I learned how to experience directly the very basis of my existence, pure consciousness, and learned how to consider and link all external phenomena as an expression of that ground field of reality through my personal experience, and expression of myself.

A summary of Maharishi's education in this respect is available at the following link:

https://en.wikipedia.org/wiki/
Transcendental_Meditation_in_education

Two years later, after being trained directly by Maharishi on a 6 months residence course, I became a teacher of TM. Once you know and experience the totality of your existence, life becomes an enjoyable journey of exploration of yourself in a very simple, spontaneous, and natural way.

We are a bit of everything (creation) and everything (creation) is a bit of us.

Q 8. Seeker: What is the difference between spiritualism and materialism? Is it right to say that where materialism ends, spiritualism begins?

Bio Yogi: In general, do not look for differences rather focus on what is common in the things that appear different. Knowing that everything is in unity, totality, and therefore indivisible in its nature. Spirituality is the reality of the matter and the matter is the reality of the spirit. You are both simultaneously that move in your own dynamism. You could not possibly say if you are matter or spirit at any point. In science, this is known as Hainzenberg's principle of uncertainty. Science could not identify an electron neither as a particle nor as a wave simultaneously at the same time. It is either particle (matter) or wave (spirit). It is a field of energy. Interestingly scientists have concluded that on that level of reality in their experiments the outcome of experiments depends on what we are looking at. The consciousness of the scientist interferes directly with that field. And if a scientist wants to see a particle the field becomes a particle. What I see I become. Otherwise, it remains a wave. The field of consciousness operates in the energy field giving rise to this universe.

Human consciousness has the potential to influence the state of the field and govern the mind/body environment aspect of life on individual and universal scales. It is an extraordinary power in each human being that allows him to create and transform using his own consciousness. From that knowledge of reality comes out all ancient systems of meditation and Yoga, all pretending to gain a ruling power over the energy field expressed as a mind and body, matter and spirit through direct experience of consciousness.

In conclusion, you are neither a body nor the mind, and you should not identify with any of them, but a universal infinite formless God consciousness that creates the forms and expresses itself through them.

What is definable is not Real

Q 9. Seeker: That means according to Hainzenberg's principle of indetermination wave is the spiritual manifestation of a particle (matter). When spiritual manifestation is realized the energy is expanded and it sends its vibrations to other particles in its field of energy. So for a man to expand his field of energy it is a must to understand and to expand the nature of his spiritual energy consciously. But the problem is that feeling of the body dominates over the awareness of being spirit. Probably that is why the material aspect overpowers man's life. This becomes the cause of suffering.

Bio Yogi: Namaskar to you.

Namaskar – means let us be together in unity without our egos. In that reality, there are no differences. Individual Ego makes one separated from his real nature. That ego is created by our individual experiences of the same reality. The ego rises on the basis of a conditioned limited mind and limited knowledge–intellect. Unlimited universal God-consciousness gets trapped, lost in its own individual form experiencing attachment, it becomes what it sees. If one sees suffering, it feels suffering. If one sees Love, it feels Love.

Consciousness in its own nature (fully awakened within itself) is the source of spirit and matter and fully independent of them. The matter is the gross, mind and spirit are the subtle, and consciousness is the subtlest level of reality. At what level of reality one is set, that level of reality he/she is going to explore and express and exchange and experience. When you go through all of them you get free from all of them and then you choose at what level you want to stay, live and act in the world. Once you are firmly established in that reality then you will not be shaken anymore by the changes in your environment.

So meditation is the way to rise and establish oneself in the truth of one's own nature as an infinite ocean of consciousness in action. Fully awaken within itself–consciousness is fully aware of itself.

Q 10:

1. What is the difference between the state of consciousness, awareness, and awakening?
2. The story of human civilizations has developed through the following phases: physical, intellectual, social, emotional, and spiritual abilities.

It is said that new paths will emerge on the roads of consciousness. Is there any further level? If yes, what? If no, then what?

Bio Yogi: Understanding this vital subject, however, implies the profound transformation of one's life on all its levels of existence. Transformation although natural requires, one's readiness and preparedness to face and cope with inner resistances and outer changes that it may cause. Generally speaking, understanding of something implies the acquisition of knowledge through experience. Knowledge is to be used and bring changes, sustain, and expand life on all its levels.

Now to your question, let us analyze it carefully: there is one "I" that "want to understand the difference". The status of the questioner (mind) is in a state of difference.

It is a common experience of human consciousness to identify, name, and see the differences (divisions) between the forms and the phenomena in life. However, the reality of existence and life is totality, indivisible and indestructible Unity, an infinite, unbounded ocean of consciousness in motion. Everything in existence, the universe and life is made out of consciousness, by the consciousness and in the consciousness. So you are and we all are basically an infinite consciousness, manifestation of it in an elaborated individual human form, like ripples of the ocean of consciousness in motion.

Individual human consciousness (manifestation or elaborated version of universal consciousness) in the state of division can never understand its own nature as Unity unless it gets a direct experience of it. So this is a starting point to understand. Everything else becomes quite easy to understand. When you are sleeping (deep sleep state of individual consciousness), you are unconscious, an-awakened and unaware of anything including your physical and mental existence. During that period of time, however, you are immersed in the ocean of infinite consciousness, intelligence of the nature that takes care of all aspects of your existence, making you a new and fueling you with the energy necessary for next day life experience. You naturally wake up at the dawn each day. Awakening means regaining a feeling of you, your existence, and recognition of everything that you have identified with, including your body image, the thought of yourself, etc. Once awakened you become aware of your environment. Being aware means reestablishing connections inwardly and outwardly allowing you to function again. The appearance of the first thought. That is a waking state of consciousness. All these states of consciousness (waking, dreaming, and sleeping) represent a continuum of self-interacting dynamism of consciousness that is a process of life and evolution of the universe. Unmanifest, formless, universal, omnipresent, and omnipotent consciousness and its manifestation in the form of universe and life, both together are one totality, one reality. From the quantum physics point of view, everything is just a unified field of energy, vibration, and frequency that manifests in the natural laws (intelligence that governs creation), the visible universe, and life in it. So consciousness in its either unmanifest or manifest, elaborated forms is a timely and timeless reality. To human beings and human intelligence as an elaborated form, a version of infinite consciousness has been entrusted with the ability to be aware of its own nature, gain knowledge, and realize the truth of Vasudhaiva Kutumbakam – the world is one family. Nature contains this basic message everywhere. Trees give fruits for the benefit of others, rivers flow for helping the growth of the trees, and cows give milk to others. So, also our lives are for helping others. This is a new path that emerges on the road of consciousness.

The only hope for the future of mankind is to rise its individual consciousness to its cosmic state– Vasudhaiva Kutumbakam.

- Think big.
- Think of everything beautiful for you and your world.
- Think of Heaven on Earth.
- Think of the elimination of poverty for the world.
- No longer should we be stuck with our little minds.
- No longer should we use our nervous system for little problems.
- We should use our nervous system for the revelations of the cosmic mind.
- Our minds should no longer be restricted to narrow boundaries, particularly the boundaries of patriotism, secularism, and religion.
- The world is a family.
- We should have in our mind that 'I own the universe', and then the universe will own us.
- We will become masters of natural law.

Through the rising of this level of understanding of consciousness, we need to globalize this wisdom of reality, unity, and truth as the only way of survival of our species through its organization as one civilization on the planet Earth. At this stage unfortunately we are not even a civilization. We are just different nation, countries that fight against each other for limited earth resources. So a vision for mankind should be first to organize itself as one planetary civilization living in harmony and peace with nature, intelligently exploring and managing its resources, respecting all other planetary life, for the benefit and evolution of life as a whole on planet earth–Vasudhaiva Kutumbakam. This should be the further level of human development that implies a complete transformation of divided human consciousness. Otherwise, we are going into the destruction of life and its future evolution.

So go by your experience and the knowledge gained through experience to give direction to your life that you choose to be the future for your children and the world they should live in the future.

Q 11. Seeker: As I have understood every human (in fact every species) exists in two forms– physical form and consciousness form. He can feel his physical existence as it does not require much effort and to fulfill its needs the body demands attention all the time, so we are busy fulfilling the needs of the body. During this process, we are fully aware of gross desires and totally unaware of our subtle requirements. It may remain so throughout life but God has designed the universe in a way that ripples at the core certainly affect every part.

Hence Supreme consciousness keeps on creating ripple effects at the subconscious level and knocks us awake from deep sleep or from a state of slumber. When we are awake, we are able to feel, see and smell our own consciousness and even get empowered to raise our consciousness to the level of supreme. This is the state where we realize unity is a source of infinity or unity is infinity. If we are not able to raise our consciousness then we are a fraction of that infinite and that implies mathematically that value may diminish to zero. If we are able to identify ourselves with the source then again mathematically, we become "§/§" which is indetermined which means unraveling of immense potential and its infinite expansion in all directions. At this stage one realizes his being as being of Him–

AHAM BRAHAMOSMI – I AM HIM

Now the question is despite knowing this we are not able to attain this. How one can progress on this path? Is knowledge sufficient to create a progressive path of consciousness with awareness in the awakened state? What are other ingredients, which can lead one to GOAL– Consciousness?

Bio Yogi: Consciousness is a life-learning subject. It is never-ending, and only expanding. Neither are you bound nor are you liberated. In fact, you are the Nature of everybody. Life exists and functions as such. Consciousness is the source, course and goal of all transformations and consequent self-introspection. So life is a continuous process of transformation of consciousness. Be aware of the process and observe it, live that process. Experience of the process gives a knowledge of it. And by the knowledge we give directions to transformation of life. However, direction can be given only by the Vision. Doesn't matter how big or small it is, if we do not have a vision then the transformation can take in any direction, at any given momentum and circumstances. Each form, from atom to the Universe, is just this chain of transformation of consciousness giving a life and human-beings are able to grasp this reality. Rely on your uniqueness, a unique expression of that process of transformation entrusted to you and by knowledge gained from experience of it, gradually you will realize the truth "I am Him"– a Ved, supreme unity consciousness already dwelling in you, its organizing power that gives orderly expressions to it.

Observe how the infinite consciousness works through you, and how it feels in you. Expand your awareness, increase your knowledge, and give desired directions to your life. Enjoy and be radiant and you will realize that you are already in the GOAL. You already have it. Nothing else is to be attained. Remember.

Q 12. Seeker: I am wondering that every transformation happens in continuity and there is nothing to be attained and we are already in Goal then why the lessons in consciousness are required? What transformation do we expect in ourselves with an aware mind? What is there which is Sahaj and Sahaj yoga?

Bio Yogi: It is a continuous chain of transformations flowing like a river. Enjoy what it is while being fully awakened. It is a thoughtless state, a ground state of awareness or mental silence (sahaj).

It could not be achieved by intellectual exercise, only by the direct regular experience of your own consciousness through meditation. This way, gradually you may increase the scope of awareness, decreasing the thoughts' presence (mind), until you are widely awake of the reality beyond your individuality. It is a natural function of the human nervous system. Then you can experience the nature of everything. Fusion. Nothing is new under the Sun.

Q 13. Seeker: Sometimes too many intellectual talks create too many thoughts in the mind and one just wants complete emptiness and nothingness. What to do in such an anxious state of mind?

Bio Yogi: You have the ultimate freedom to do with your life as you like. To fulfill its potential completely, or to make some smaller version of yourself, it all depends upon your effort and commitment.

You make the decisions to fulfill, to whatever extent, the potential life that exists within you. That is your choice. So, keep asking until you completely exhaust your intellect, mind, and body. Satisfy all your urges and desires, observe, understand and learn out from your experiences.

Intellectualizing without practicing does not create any lasting value.

If you ignore an Ant, then you are ignorant. Give your classroom students the following task. First, assign them to two equal groups.

Instruct one group to work together and describe all the differences they are able to identify between humans and ants. Instruct a second group to identify all that is similar between the human species and ants. Let each group work separately for 20 minutes and then their representatives should announce in front of all, their findings and conclusions. Then they have to define a common ground of understanding of the issue.

General guidelines: Ants and humans are the forms of the same universe, made of the same stuff, constituents, consciousness, atoms and molecules, amino acids, proteins tissues, and organs, living on the same planet Earth, sharing the same space and resources. They are both born and they perish as well. They live in organized structures colonies (ants) societies (humans). They both communicate within their species in specific ways, and they take care of their progeny, and so on. It is the aim of this exercise that students become aware of the fact that we are part of an intelligent and organized ecosystem of nature in the same way as the ants, whose existence is neglected by us unless they bite us. So students can practice watching in their daily life not to step on an ant whenever they walk. You can design and create similar assignments in many different ways that can progressively increase the awareness of the students and their understanding of themselves, their society, their environment, nature and the universe.

- When you observe you are anxious and set back.
- Beyond individuality is universality,
- Beyond individual being is a cosmic, universal being,
- Beyond individual consciousness is universal, infinite consciousness,
- Beyond the noise and agitation is the silence.

So, practice silence regularly twice a day for 15-20 minutes, in the morning and in the afternoon. Silence is a ground state of our existence and consciousness. Everything comes out and goes back into silence. So why not practice it and find out how we function?

Reserve a fixed time of the day routinely for yourself in a silent place. Sit comfortably, close your eyes, and just do nothing. Just watch, and observe what is going on in you. Naturally, you will observe the activity of your mind as a thought process and the activity of your body as breathing, heart beating, etc. Do not analyze your thoughts, nor try to fight them out. Just notice their presence. If they are bothering you, direct your attention to your breath. Observe your breath cycle. Try to do this regularly for a few days and then write to me about your experiences with any questions that you may have.

Q 14. What is the most powerful success mantra that teachers may impart to their students? Through our education system, we always nurture the thought that "you shall be best. Your result will be excellent. You will get admission to the best college. You shall get the best job......"

Everywhere, it is you and, not people around you, not the environment around you, not thoughts around you, not goodness around you. Is it accurate that the first step to success is material accomplishment, and then one can gradually progress towards comprehension of subtle existence, exploring subtle identity, developing subtle awareness, and hence self-realization?

Is there a set path to success? Is there an alternative form of success?

Bio Yogi: Tell them to be happy. "Be Happy" is the mantra. Whatever they think, say, or do in their lives, they should always ask the simple question "Am I a happy person"? Ask them to listen to the answer coming from within. Material and spiritual, manifest and unmanifest, thought and matter, gradually rise together as a movement (waves) of one undivided nature of consciousness in motion. We are an amalgam of spirit and matter existing together, dancing, balancing and influencing each other all the time. It is an infinite consciousness that awakens, creates thoughts, and manifests in its own nature as a mind and a body (individual or universal). An individual is cosmic, and cosmic is an individual. How could there possibly be a distinction?

Only in ignorance, existence, consciousness, bliss does one forget his true essence.

Everybody should live and experience the totality of their nature on both sides. Existential levels, spiritual as well as material are in balance and harmony, leading to an awareness of peace and consonance across the universe.

Tell your students that they should be glorious and victorious in their thoughts, words and actions free of strains and stresses.

There is no set path to success.

Everyone is a unique expression of the universe (from ants to human beings). One should not compare and compete with others. Simply be and express who you already are: a total, complete, indivisible, and unique expression of the universe.

Let the universe express and manifest itself wholly through you.

That is a success. Do not oppose and do not create obstacles to the natural flow of life and the intelligence that already exists in you.

Q 15. Are the goals of life different from the purpose of life?

Goals, I believe, can be accomplished but, purpose defines the course of life and imparts vitality. The purpose is lived with every breath of life, and it may give directions to goals, energy to achieve the goals, and expand one to submerge in the infinite. Purpose can always help us decide on new goal, and choose new paths....Purpose cannot be accomplished; it can just be lived.

- Should the goal of life be different from the purpose of life?
- Should the goals of life for an 18-year boy or girl be different from those of a person of 40 years of age or a person of 70 years of age?
- What should be the purpose of life for people of different ages? How can one sense it? Most of the time, we are ignorant about such things.
- How the youth can be sensitized and prepared for such issues?

Bio Yogi: "Concerns and the quest of youth...", What should be the goal and purpose of life?

Basically, there is no such a thing as a predefined goal and purpose to attain. All we have in life are merely necessities. We all grow (individually and historically), striving to meet our needs (basic or higher), every level of our individual or collective existence whether they are biological, psychological, sociological, or spiritual. That's how we accumulate the experience and knowledge that gives us a sense of meaning and feeling in life and defines our individual and collective goals and purposes. We grow through desires (goals) and beliefs (purposes), striving to fulfill them. The nature of life, however, is continuity and intensity.

In an effort to meet our needs (through desires), we simply want to assure continuity of existence (individual or collective). All we are interested in, is to assure continuity and intensity of life experience and beliefs. In other words, the physical and the biological aspect of our existence ensure the continuity of the supports (forms of life) throughout evolution, which finally empowers our species with the ability to manifest and reflect the intensity of the experience of higher consciousness, through beliefs (purposes).

To put it simply, individuals (needy) should satisfy their needs harnessing and unfolding their own abilities inherent in them by nature. Otherwise, we become greedy (individually or collectively). Our desires and beliefs, as well as our goals and purposes determine the trajectory of our life. Desires arise from the thought process, and the beliefs from a sense of "I" consciousness, identity. So everybody (irrespective of age and beliefs) should study Consciousness, the very self of our being that links us inseparably with the universe. The youth should be prepared and sensitized through Vedic Education. Vedic education is the only education that can bring understanding and fulfillment of all goals and purposes. So one should grow by establishing the truth that he is a creator and the master of his own creation. In this way, the goals meet the purposes, and the desires are guided by beliefs in harmony. Otherwise, we are played and victimized (individually or collectively) by false or manipulated desires and beliefs, goals, and purposes.

In conclusion, a youth should listen, study, reflect and understand, recognize and practice, and finally use the fruits of knowledge achieved by their own effort. This will make them fulfilled and happy with any purpose or goal that they may have set up for themselves.

Q 16. Seeker: Vedic education holds different connotations for different people. What is your concept of Vedic education?

Bio Yogi: To solve any problem in life, we need knowledge. The biggest problem arises from the fact that we do not know who we are, why we are here, and where we will go.

Vedic education provides knowledge of consciousness and technology for its upliftment. Basically, it is education centered on oneself. A main subject is the Self with all its forms and aspects of existence like mathematics, physics, chemistry, biology, sociology, cosmology, and consciousness.

Q 17: Vedic Education system encourages questioning. All the Upanishads started with questions from the disciples. Why is the questioning important?

Bio Yogi: Questioning increases awareness and the sharpness of the mind. So keep questioning. Repeat the same question again and again. Questioning is a probe into oneself and brings self-knowledge. Awareness is the key. Be aware of awareness. Awareness happens only if one is fully awakened by the unbounded ocean of consciousness in motion. Only when consciousness is fully awakened within itself can it fully know itself. When consciousness knows itself and structures in two values: the knower and the known. It polarises, not divides. Everything in creation is in a polarised state.

When the knower understands the known dynamics of thoughts, a mental aspect of consciousness is created. The process of knowledge, knowingness, the intellect aspect of consciousness, and a flow of consciousness i.e. the creation of the universe. Ego, I am a Brahman, are all components of thought dynamics. As a result, there is only one universal consciousness that can be experienced on both levels manifest (universe, individual consciousness) and unmanifest (transcendental, universal consciousness). Unmanifest, universal consciousness is hidden and expressed in the manifest (from the atom to the universe), and the manifest, universeis made of unmanifest, universal consciousness. Be mindful of both individual and universal values, refrain from loosing unity in the face of polarised values, i.e., diversity. So that is Lila, a cosmic play. Its hides and wants to be seen. Whatever the manifest forms, including human beings do, is because of this unmanifest tendency within that want to be seen. This is why so many beauties, colors, forms, sounds, etc., can be seen and experienced in creation. In creation, everything and everyone desires to be seen and identified.

Rise and fall are imagined in the ocean of consciousness in motion. You are already that, which you are desperately seeking. Like a fish is seeking an ocean while being an ocean. As a fish feels in the ocean the ocean feels in the fish.

If the sky can be seen in your eyes, it is because you are seen from the sky. If the Atman can be realized by the Jeev, it is because the jeev is the reflection of the Atman.

3

An Evening with Indian Seekers

Welcome dinner was organized by Mr. Naveen Goswami at St. Margret School, Prashant Vihar, Delhi. Ceremony started with meditation followed by a talk by Mr Milovan Stankov. He was addressing the galaxy of seekers in quest of truth.

He started his talk with a note asking people present there whether they are still left with more than four questions in life. Everyone pondered. With hearty laughter, he continued that there are only four basic questions of the truth of life and if one gets to know and experience their answers, then they can be the 'Master of his life'. The questions are:

- Who am I?
- What is the purpose of my existence?
- How I am connected to the universe?
- What is the true relation between Jeev, jagat and Atma?

Mr. Milovan tried to answer these questions of seekers.

He said that every I is part of this universe and that each one of us is a universe, an infinite universe with the same energy. And that means one God expressed in infinite individuals. We shall understand that idea of God actually propagates the idea of oneness with this creation and not the idea of one being existing in isolation or infinite ones.

He further added that if we start appreciating ourselves as part of the universe and hence as part of HIM then we will very clearly understand that the sole purpose of our existence is creation or to be the Master of creation. Our life is a journey of acquiring Mastery in the skill of creating and being aware of it.

Creation in thoughts, actions, and perception helps one to create new designs and new patterns of existing paradigms. Creation always leads to the evolution of self, society, and the universe.

He further added that each one of us is already evolved but we are not able to understand this. To understand this we shall be consciously aware of the concepts built in our minds due to our experience or perceptions. We shall analyze our concepts around the contexts. This contextualization of our own concepts decides our course of life and makes us able to have conscious choices.

Our choices make us happy or sad, joyful or sorrowful, satisfied or frustrated……., because our choices are our contract with God. What we sign in our full consciousness with God is what we receive as per the contract.

The question is "How we can sign a good contract with God or that Param-Atma".

We need to know that Pran –Atma is our own Atma or soul in the highest form of the awakened state. One is awake when one is sensitive toward the existence of every jeev in the surrounding. One is awake when one is concerned with the welfare of every jeev and hence about the welfare of the whole world. One is awake when one is always in an attention state i.e. in the tension of stitching all bonds which connect us at a subtle level. One is awake when one is aware of oneself as matter and spirit both. One is awake when one internalizes the truth of "Aham tattvamasi" (I am Thee) Knowledge of this truth and believing in this.

Truth is the answer to all questions raised in the beginning.

(One can attain this knowledge through Meditation and Devotion. He emphasized the word 'devotion' as it is the invisible force that drives everyone in the realization of anything.)

St. Margret School,
Prashant Vihar, New Delhi

Report, 12 June 2017

4

Bond of Transcendental Love and Silence with Maharishi Mahesh Yogi and Tapovani Ma

– Milovan

I was born in Serbia, surrounded by mountains and strikingly beautiful Nature. Being in the midst of Nature, mingling with the mountains, the river, the animals, the birds, and the flora, I started thinking about them. Right from childhood, having lived amidst nature, I was connected with animals and insects in such a way that I started studying Biology at the age of nine. I started studying and learned the correct way of understanding life, its intricacies, and its psychology. I graduated with a degree, but the exploration continued. With further education, I came in contact with many books of which some Indian books on their culture and philosophy threw more light on my understanding of Nature and Life. With this, my thirst increased.

It appears to me, that wherever we may be born, the influence of our surroundings is deeply ingrained in us. After this, the Soul strengthens that culture through its work, and the Divine makes it an easy path. There was no probability of me coming here from the West. It is not that the Himalayas have drawn me here. I was born amidst snow-capped mountains. I opened my eyes to the splendor of the mountains. The seed of Spirituality is sown within by birth. A conducive environment nurtures it, but is stifled by an unfavorable atmosphere. The eternal Indian culture and its values– the holy men, the yogis– brought out an insatiable thirst to meet them.

It was after this that I read Maharshi Mahesh Yogi's philosophy, and the state of emptiness gave way to fullness. When Maharshi

Mahesh Yogi came to the West for the first time in 1963, I became a part of his Movement and immersed myself in knowing the Self.

I have met Maharishi in person several times since 1981 before starting my TM teacher training course, and then regularly in Switzerland and Holland until February 2008, when Maharishi passed away.

For the very first time in August of 1981, at the Maharishi's Capitol in Selisberg (Switzerland), I saw Maharishi's appearance as a sparkling speaking silence in absolute stillness. An auspicious, astonishing feeling that opens an existing inner space where I was always been instinctively rescued from the outside world. My communication with Maharishi was always on that ground of silence, intuitive, with few a words here and there. Maharishi's words always resonate as a clear visual realization inside me, and the ever-lasting silence whispering inwardly has become my primary nature ever since.

The Maharishi's imprint of that lively silence made a dynamic continuum of myself resonate, vibrantly unveiling the everlasting existence of ultimate reality in me as the only solid ground of understanding offered to human beings through Vedic wisdom: "Brahma Satyam Jagat Mithya Jiva Brahmaiva Naparah".

I feel that when one immerses and entwines oneself in growing closer to God, either in knowledge or in devotion, and walks this path, then it is an easy road. When the moment is ready, time takes to the right destination. This happened to me too. The resulting good deeds of my past life were instrumental in bringing me to India and reaching me to the holy saints of the Himalayas. The journey that began twenty-five years ago is still on. To know me, to reach the deeper states of consciousness; Tapovan was the acme. I spent a fortnight every year in Tapovan. When I learned that Mother Subadra was there for nine years, and the urge to meet her brought me to Dharali. After this, my journey to Tapovan and the journey to see the Mother became an annual pilgrimage. Whatever I gained through knowledge, in Tapovan, I tried to understand and put into practice. The Mother did the same. Whatever she gained in the first five to six decades of her life she put it into practice in the solitude of Tapovan. Now she shares all that she gained there. She dedicated her life to service of the seekers of truth, Jiganasus, and aspirants of truth. She knew what her goal was, and that service was the path. During our first meeting with her, we didn't even know when she cooked for us all the while, I saw her moving around us! That day has remained memorable for me when she sang devotional songs, danced with us, and enveloped us with her love. It was from this time on this journey that a new chapter of closeness grew between us. We returned home with memories of her. After this, when we visited India, Tapovan, we would meet with the Mother. Every meeting with her, awakened in us a new experience. As soon as we met her a spark would ignite instantly. Whatever the condition one would be in, all fatigue and worries would vanish, leaving one relaxed. Everything would melt away. She is a universal being, that none would return without being influenced.

I come annually to India, stay with the Mother, visit Tapovan, and sit in her cave. Both in France and in India, people wonder how I have managed the relationship with the Mother (Subhdra Ma) for more than two decades despite me not knowing Hindi or her, French. I feel that understanding surpasses language and is not an impediment, manifesting itself through work. The conversation between us is through our hearts.

My relationship with Mother Subadhra is comparable to that between two souls, between two hearts; between an innocent child and its mother. A child's needs are fulfilled in time without even asking for it.

I participate in the festivities of the 'Narayana family' at Gangotri Ashram. The truth is that these visits have led to the strengthening of the bond between us year after year.

Whatever crossed the mind of the Mother, I would become instrumental in its fulfillment, even without being told. Whether it be a temple for Narayan or the image of a child Hanuman's pinnacle, the wish of the Mother was completed to the tee. My wife and my children have also been blessed in her presence. At the installation of Child Hanuman and the festivities, my wife, dressed in Indian attire participated in all the rituals. The seed of devotion sown by the Mother, through affection, love, and concern, embedded itself deep within me and my family, Westerners, and has blossomed and borne fruit in France. Today, my house in France is a temple devoted to Yoga, and a cave within has an idol of Shiva."

5

Introspection of Self Post-India Visit

About India Shared by Family Members of Milovan

The natural splendour and impression of India will remain with me iternally. Indian possesses the ability to captivate and enchant people with smiles everywhere around us.

The silence of the Himlayas, the force of the Ganges, the luscious mangoes, the smiling eyes, the scrims, the eternal hues of the saris, and how everyone called me Mataji as I walked through India's streets sculpted my emotions and thoughts into something unfathomable.

–Slavica Petrovic (Milovan's sister)

*** *** ***

Travelling is now more than just sightseeing; it is a profound and long-lasting change in one's outlook towards life. This journey to India has been the most tranformatic for me thus far since it makes me value and appreciate everything.

– Stankov Ortiz, Daughter of Bio-Yogi
student of Medicine at Paris

*** *** ***

I believe this trip has helped me a lot to overcome my emotions and make peace with myself. When I think of the time I spent in India, it brings back very warm feelings of connection with nature, and with a culture that is totally fascinating and different from my own. It was a real shock. But a very positive and powerful one that definitely impacted who I am today. Learning the difference, learning what's important, and opening yourself to experiencing the unknown. A spiritual journey for the mind the body and the heart. It was the first time that I truly felt free.

This experience was very enriching spiritually and I learned a lot about myself through meditation and introspection. If there is one thing that I could take out from my experience in India is that happiness doesn't mean possession. I learned to detach myself more from materialism and to appreciate other things like the company of a loved one, the warmth of the sun on a cold winter day, or the sound of the birds in the morning. I learned to be more aware of what is around me, and live more in the moment.

Om Namah Shivaya !!!!!

–Luka Stankov the son of Bio-Yogi Milovan

***   ***   ***

People are so special and kind, I learned what real happiness is, how humble and honest people are and how powerful their emotions are. India has been the most beautiful country I ever experienced, the culture is deeply entrenched. The people are so special, their traditions, how elders are so respected, how the family is always first, how united they are. I wish I could have something similar.

For me India means happiness.

–Kelly, Daughter of Bio-Yogi,
student of Psychology in Medellin, Colombia

***   ***   ***

All the experiences I had in India have helped me to be an open-minded person and to see life in my own way. India is a unique country, we could even say that it is another universe in comparison to France.

–Milovan Stankov-Pugès, second son of Bio-Yogi

***   ***   ***

I was stripped away of all of the superficial Western comfort and lifestyle. This Journey transformed me profoundly, opened my mind, and made me realize that the true values of lifeare family bonding, générosity, introspection, simplicity, and humility.

– Marko

*** *** ***

No electricity, no mobile phone, no internet, it was a little bit hard for me at first, I mean Iam young and I need all these things, then I have to find out how to pass the time because in a place like Tapovan, it's just you and nature and you discover how much you can talk to yourself and I think that this is a way to discover a little bit more about yourself.

–Simon

*** *** ***

It was so obvious to me how versatile Indian culture is and I quickly grasped on a very high level the depth of the knowledge present in India. As knowledge is now available to all of us through rectangle devices we keep in our pockets, I quickly learned that one of the keys is a proper understanding of the knowledge.

–Aleksandar Stankov

*** *** ***

6

Impressions by Indian Seekers

This picture is from the time when I first met Brother Milovan. I was initially introduced to him by his wife. She happened to listen to my concert in Belgrade and took my photo and showed it to Milovan, and they kept my photo in their meditation room. Milovan organized a couple of concerts in 1997, and I went to France with my three accompanying artists. In the first meeting itself, he addressed me as a sister and since, then he has become a real brother to me. Not only me but my entire family has now become attached to him and his family.

The unique thing about him is that being born in Serbia, and settled in France, and how he embraced Indian spirituality and his knowledge of the Vedas is amazing. He is a thoroughly disciplined person who spends and enjoys hours of meditation. He is a strict vegetarian and comes to the Himalayas every year to rejuvenate himself.

There is so much to write about him, but in a sentence, he is an ideal and standing example for the youth and for all generations of the world.

–Padamshri Sumitra Guha
(a renowned classical singer)

***   ***   ***

Milovan Stankov - Zero Complaining

The most unique quality that I have experienced in Milovan, after knowing him for the past many years, is that he remains in One state of mind. The unified, the stable, the unwavering; what we call is eternal also.

And to add to it, I always feel amazed to see him appreciating and eating each and every food item offered to him with utmost joy and relishing it in totality without any complaints, any inhibition.

Whenever he comes to India, many of our friends who wish to gain from his knowledge and experience, invite him to their homes and serve him different types of Indian delicacies, which he eats with gratitude. He only has words of appreciation and blessings.

I have never seen him complain a bit regarding anything, regarding any situation, as if everything is happening according to his wish or his wish, is so airy, so light that it enters each situation and becomes one. He flows with the flow and enjoys the present moment joyously.

One also feels blessed in his company.

–Bindu Popli (Painter)
Bindu Art Aura

*** *** ***

फ्रांस के वैज्ञानिक मिलोवन स्टेनकोव विज्ञान और योग का संगम है। विगत् 30 वर्षो से निरंतर हिमालय में गहन साधना करने आते है। वैदिक ज्ञान को इन्होंने अपने में समा लिया है। जीवन, अध्यातम और विज्ञान – इन तीनों के मध्य जो तालमेल होना चाहिए; उसकी इन्हें गहरी समझ है।

भारतीय मनीषा के महामंत्र 'वसुधैव कुटुंबकम' को ये सदा अपने साथ लेकर चलते हैं। सौभाग्यशाली हैं वे लोग जिन्हें इनसे कुछ सीखने का अवसर प्राप्त हुआ है।

।। तन्मेमनः शिव संकल्पस्तु ।।

–स्वामी ईशान महेश
EeshaanDhyanMandir.com

7

Newspaper Clippings

The Hindu
BUSINESS LINE
Wednesday, July 16, 1997

Veda Lab to launch TB detection kit

Somasekhar Mulugu
NEW DELHI, July 15

INSPIRED by the ancient Indian texts — Vedas, a Yugoslav-born biologist, Mr. Milovan Stankov, in collaboration with Dr. Raphael Donati, launched a pharma company called Veda Lab on the outskirts of Paris in 1991.

Specialising in the development of immunodiagnostic tests and kits, the company has come up with a variety of products for hepatitis B, pregnancy detection kits, tumour markers and hormones.

Now, the $ 8-million French company plans to launch its latest product — a rapid single-step detection test for tuberculosis in India. It has tied-up with Ajanta agencies, part of the Nobel group of industries, New Delhi to market it from September.

The Chief Executive Officer of Veda Lab, Mr. Milovan Stankov, told *Business Line* that the product is based on colloidal gold technology with immuno-chromatographic methodology on membrane support. In simple terms the kit analyses a single drop of blood from the patient. In a matter of 10 minutes it will give the result. If the patient has TB it is indicated by two bands and if he does not by a single band.

The advantage of this quick detection kit is, anybody can perform it. Its shelf-life is nearly two years and the detection can be made at a very early stage of infection, Mr. Stankov said. The test is also very economical, he claimed.

The TB detection kit developed in November, 1996 has already been launched in South Africa, Russia and Thailand. "We have plans to go to China this year", he said.

Veda Lab introduced a similar one-step surface antigen based test for the detection of hepatitis B in the country a couple of years ago. The company spends about 10 per cent of its turnover on research and development annually, Mr. Stankov added.

Mr. Stankov said diagnostics in the area of veterinary (animal diseases), agro products (quality of food products) and environment (water quality) and Allergy would be the focus of research for the Lab in the coming years.

"India has tremendous knowledge among its people and ancient texts and this is the reason which brings me every year to visit the Himalayas and meet people", says Mr. Stankov, who is a disciple of Maharshi Mahesh Yogi and quotes from the Bhagwad Gita. In fact the company's brochure cites a quotation from the text.

Mr. Rajesh Maheshwari, Vice-President (Operations) of Noble Group, said that during the first year of agreement the kits would be imported and sold in the market. Later, we would be keen of having production facilities in the country.

2 DELHI TIMES . THE TIMES OF INDIA THURSDAY AUGUST 21 1997

A compact kit for early detection of TB

India has the dubious distinction of housing one-third of the world's tuberculosis patients with 15 million infected people. In other words 1.5 per cent of India's population suffers from the disease implying that the TB menace has to be tackled on a war footing. The first step towards curbing the spread of TB is early detection.

Milovan Stankov, President and Director General, Veda. Lab, a French company, was in the capital to finalise the introduction of a Tuberculosis detection kit —a rapid immunodiagnostic test for detection of antikoch's bacillus antibodies in Serum\Plasma.

The company which was formed in 1991 specialises in the manufacture of rapid immunodiagnostic tests and has introduced 30 immunodiagnostic kits the world over including the Hepatitis B check and pregnancy test kits, which have been available in the country for a couple of years now.

The advantages of the ten-minute TB test kit are that it can detect the presence of tuberculosis bacillus within a week of infection. According to Stankov, a follower of Maharshi

Milovan Stankov

Mahesh Yogi for the past 20 years who spends three weeks in India every year meditating in the Himalayas, the added advantages of the kit are "a long shelf life, no instrumentation and the fact that the test can be conducted anywhere.

The kit is very stable because of the dry chemistry which is suited to the Indian environment. A clinical evaluation reveals high specifity and sensitivity."

Veda. Lab's TB detection kit which was introduced in Europe and the United States in November 1996, has already been made available to laboratories and doctors throughout the country.

Though Veda. Lab products have been available in the country, so far they were being marketed under the Original Equipment Manufacturers (OEM) label. With the TB kit, the company with a turnover of US $ 8 million, is entering the Indian market with the Veda. Lab label. The kit will be marketed by Ajanta Agency (P) Ltd, a company which has been floated under the flagship of the Noble Group.

With roughly 15 lakh fresh cases of TB being detected every year, the market is "approximately 10 million kits per year", says Rajesh Maheshwari, Vice President (Operations), Noble Group.

Veda.Lab has plans of introducing the veterinary diagnosis kits, which have already been introduced in the West, environmental diagnosis kits and agro-alimentary diagnosis kits in India at a later stage.

Stankovis an Yugoslavian who studied biologybut moved on to psychology which he studied only for a year because he found it very boring.

In 1991, he set up Veda. Lab, an R & Dmanufacturing company of immunodiagnostic tests and kits with Dr Raphael Donati.

THE PIONEER

July 24, 1997

10 QUESTIONS

For instant results

Vedalab is entering India with its Tuberculosis Rapid Immuno-diagnostic Test Kit. Milovan Stankov, President-CEO, speaks to **Krishna Nath** about the magic potion

Q1. When was Vedalab established and for what purpose?

A. Vedalab was created in July 1991 under the aegis of Dr Raphael Donati, President COO and myself as President CEO. The company specialises in research, development, production and marketing of rapid immuno-diagnostic tests using immuno-chromatographic principles. The company is located at ZAT du Londeau of Alencon city in France. We produce over 1 million tests per month, using our own production technology.

Q2. What is the new product that you are launching?

A. Our new product is for the early detection of an active infection of tuberculosis. The main features of this technology is that it is simple to use, gives a qualitative result in a few minutes and is very economical. The test requires no instrumentation or specialised personnel. All components of the test are incorporated into the dry immuno-chemistry format so that nothing else is needed to perform the test except one drop of finger prick blood, serum or plasma.

Q3. How does the system really work?

A. It is a simple process and can be done at home or at the hospital. It contains a plastic device with one 'well' where you apply one drop of blood or serum/plasma and a few drops of the diluent separately. After 10 minutes, the result will develop in the form of visually-distinguishable red coloured lines. If there are two lines appearing, it means the person is carrying an active infection of TB. If there is one line appearing, i.e. the control line, it means the test is negative.

Q4. Is it the first time you are launching your tuberculosis test kit in India?

A. Yes. The kit has been jointly developed with another French company which is involved in tuberculosis antigen purification and both the companies have independent rights for distributing this product in India.

Q5. What kind of distribution network do you have in India?

A. We have agreed on a general single import point strategy with Noale Group and Ajanta Agency who will be distributing the kit all over India. In India, going by the official statistics, about 100,000 such cases occur every year. We believe a simple technology like this can help detect the disease at an early stage and thus reduce its incidence.

Q6. Can it be adopted as a personal test kit by individuals?

A. In some countries like Russia they have adopted this kit as a home test. A person can go to a pharmacy and buy the kit and test himself. It is upto our representatives here to decide how they want to position the product in India. However, for starters, it will be targeted at hospitals, clinics, and rural laboratories.

Q7. What is the price of the TB kit?

A. The cost price will be adjusted to the marketing needs. It is our aim to adopt a price that will be affordable to everyone.

Q8. What kind of marketing network does Vedalab have worldwide?

A. We operate mainly through OEM distributors spread across 80 countries. In Europe, beside France, Vedalab is selling in Germany, Italy, Spain, Sweden, Norway, Greece and Turkey. We are quite successful in Asia, Saudi Arabia, the US, Canada, Colombia, Mexico, Argentina, Brazil, Singapore, Hong Kong, Taiwan, Thailand, Malaysia and Australia too. We are making a strong effort in the Eastern European countries Poland, Slovakia, Ukraine, Russia, Hungary, Bulgaria and Yugoslavia.

Q9. What is the present growth rate of the company?

A. The company's business volume has grown from $1 million in 1992 to $8 million in 1996, clearly demonstrating Vedalab's right approach to the market and its customers.

Q10. What are the grants and awards received by the company?

A. For its contribution to innovative immuno-diagnostic research, Vedalab received $40,000 in 1991 and $100,000 in 1993 from the French Industrial Authorities. Besides, Vedalab has been awarded twice for its export excellence by 'Trophee de l'Exportation' in 1994 and 1996 and for its exceptional results in 1995 by 'Trophee des Espoirs de l'Economie.'

Evening News Aug. 16, 1997

KNOWLEDGE IS HEALTH

TUBERCLOSIS is one of the most dreaded disease and its early detection can help in curing the disease. Veda Lab has recently launched a rapid test kit in India for early detection of an active infection of tuberculosis. It is compact and easy to use, gives qualitative result in a few minutes. The test requires no instrumentation or specialised personnel. All components of the tests are incorporated into the dry immuno-chemistry format. It involves a simple process which can be done at home.

Imbibing cultural differences

A cultural exchange programme was organised at **SD Public School, Pitampura**. Milovan Stankov, a scientist and Estella, a student of L'assomption School from France visited the school. A documentary on how India was bathed in different colours of caste, creed, culture and religion was showcased to the guests.

Acrobatic and rhythmic yoga moves by students enthralled the guests. A French song was presented by students on environment concerns. Estella shared a presentation in detail about French culture and civilisation. She talked about the difference between Indian and French education. Milovan addressed the students and answered their queries. He stressed on the importance of meditation and spiritualism in students' life.

School principal Anita Sharma thanked the guests and urged students to follow the right path of moral values and discipline. It was a learning experience and a unique platform where students imbibed cultural and traditional difference between India and France.

A student exchange programme was designed by Christelijk College Nassau-Veluwe, Netherlands, for the students of **St Mark's Girls Sr Sec School, Meera Bagh** and Copernicus Upper Secondary, Poland. A delegation of eight students of class-IX and two teachers, Anjali Handa and Jasjit Kaur Mehta visited Harderwijk, Netherlands.

The students participated in the interactive sessions for the project World War-II. Besides the academics and cultural lessons, they also visited a few places of interest. The students were taken on a guided tour of Harderwijk city, a walk through the city of Amsterdam where they saw the Jewish historical museum and the National Art Gallery. They walke through the woods of Kamp Westerbork and Verscholen Dorp, sav the Hetloo Palace and spent a evening at Giethoorn. Durin their stay, they performed the foll dance of Punjab and also wit nessed a theatre show by th Dutch students. The students go an opportunity to meet Piet Edelman, an eye-witness of World War II, during an interview session.

The exchange programme provided a unique and fruitful learning experience through which the students understood the meaning of freedom and liberation.